# HANDLE WITH CARE

## Emotions, Finance, Sexuality

LEADER'S GUIDE

FOCUS FAMILY

TYNDALE HOUSE PUBLISHERS, INC.
Carol Stream, Illinois

# CONTENTS

# WELCOME!

Marriage can be tough—but learning about it doesn't have to be. In fact, we think you'll find this course easy to use, to the point—even fun.

At the heart of each session is a DVD presentation featuring some of today's top marriage experts.

Then there's the Participant's Guide—the book each of your group members will need to make the course personal.

Finally, there's the Leader's Guide—the book you're holding right now. It's designed to help you turn the DVD and Participant's Guide into a lively group experience in which spouses learn and support each other.

## Preparing for the Session

Before each meeting, review the session plan in this book. Look at the corresponding chapter in the Participant's Guide. Preview the DVD segment if possible; then make sure it's cued up for your group to watch.

For most sessions, you'll need pencils or pens. For some, if your group is large, you may need chalkboard and chalk or other display surface and writing tool (newsprint and marker, white board and marker, etc.). You may also need to gather a few other easy-to-find materials, listed in "Setting the Stage" at the start of each session.

## Leading the Session

You'll find the session plans easy to follow. Instructions to you are in regular type; things you might say to the group are in bold type; suggested answers are in parentheses.

Each session, designed to last about an hour, includes five steps:

*1. Getting Together (5 minutes)*
Using a game or other "icebreaker" activity, you'll grab the group's interest and build a sense of community. This step is optional; if your group members need help getting acquainted, or if they just like to have a good time, it can be especially valuable.

*2. Finding Yourself (5-10 minutes)*
Participants take a survey to help them see how this session topic might benefit them.

*3. Catching the Vision (20-25 minutes)*
Watch and discuss the DVD segment.

*4. Digging Deeper (10 minutes)*
If part of your group's mission is discussing God's Word, you'll want to include this Bible study step. If yours is more of a community outreach effort, you may wish to condense or delete this section.

*5. Making It Work (10 minutes)*
It's time for practical application, as group members use the corresponding section of the Participant's Guide to come up with action plans for their own marriages.

*6. Bringing It Home (5 minutes)*
For you, this is a brief wrap-up. For group members, it's something to read later: practical advice from a counselor.

## Tips for Success

- If your group is like most, you often run out of time before you run out of discussion questions and activities. What to do? Simply choose the exercises and questions you think will be most helpful to your group and concentrate on those. Try starting with the bare essentials—watching the DVD and applying the principles through the "Making It Work" activity—and add steps as your schedule allows.
- Invite discussion, but don't be surprised if some group members are reluctant to share personal information. If people want to reflect silently on a probing question, encourage them to do so.
- Couples will benefit most, of course, if both spouses attend your sessions. In some cases, though, schedules or interest levels may require some spouses to attend alone. If that's true in your group, be sure to help these individuals feel welcomed and supported. You'll need to adapt some activities in this guide accordingly. Instead of having spouses discuss a question, for example,

you may want to form subgroups of three to five—or simply skip questions that would be too personal for individuals to discuss with anyone other than a mate.

- Don't allow laughter at anyone's expense. If some of the discussion questions seem likely to cause embarrassment, feel free to omit them; if they would be more appropriately answered between husband and wife in private, encourage group members to do so later.

- Instead of pressing group members to reveal information they're not comfortable sharing, tell an occasional story on yourself if you like. Propose the following guidelines to participants: Before raising a question or referring to an experience, make sure it won't embarrass your spouse; if in doubt, privately ask your spouse's permission beforehand; maintain confidentiality.

- Let participants know that if they're struggling in their marriages, help is available. Provide contact information for local Christian counselors, especially any who are connected with your church. If your church staff doesn't know of a therapist, Focus on the Family has a referral network of Christian counselors. For information, call 1-800-A-FAMILY and ask for the counseling department. You can also download free, printable brochures offering help for couples at http://www.focusonthefamily.com/marriage/articles/brochures.aspx.

- If possible, each group member—not just each couple—should have a Participant's Guide. Otherwise, spouses won't be able to write individual responses to opinion questions. It's a good idea to have a few extra copies of the participant's guide on hand, so that visitors (and those who forgot their books) can take part.

- If you don't have an answer to every question, join the club! It's okay to say, "I don't know." Ask group members to share wisdom from their experience. Refer people to books like *Complete Guide to the First Five Years of Marriage* (Focus on the Family/Tyndale House, 2006), which contains help for almost any stage of married life.

- Have a good time! Marriage may be serious business, but most of your group members probably would appreciate a light touch as they learn. Let your group be a place where spouses can laugh together and gain perspective on their marital challenges.

- Pray. Pray for your group members during the week. Urge them to pray for each other. Ask God to help each person become the loving, effective mate he or she was meant to be.

For additional tips on leading your group, see the "Instructions for Leaders" feature on the DVD. You can also find further advice for your couples at focusonthefamily.com/marriage.

Ready to have a lasting, positive impact on the marriages represented in your group? May God bless you as you lead!

**Note:** Many issues addressed in this series are difficult ones. Some couples may need to address them in greater detail and depth. The DVD presentations and this guide are intended as general advice only, and not to replace clinical counseling, medical treatment, legal counsel, or financial guidance.

Session 1

# ONE STEP AT A TIME

In this DVD segment, Drs. John Trent and Greg Smalley present a little idea that gets big results: improving your marriage a step at a time instead of trying to leap the Grand Canyon in a single bound.

Small changes are doable—and they work. In fact, it's the little things that often make the difference between couples who do well and those who struggle. Making minor, frequent course corrections on your marital journey prevents panicky, wrenching attempts at change later. And when it comes to changing your spouse, keep your expectations small, too.

## Session Aim
To help group members improve their marriages by making small, relatively easy "course corrections" instead of insisting on major, more difficult changes that are less likely to happen.

## Setting the Stage
- Read this session plan and Chapter 1 in the Participant's Guide.
- Provide pencils or pens.
- Bring a team prize if you want to award one for the contest in Step 1.
- Cue up the DVD to segment 1, "One Step at a Time."

## Optional Icebreaker
*(5 minutes)*

Here's a fun way to get started—and introduce the subject at the same time.

Form teams; give each team a piece of paper and pen or pencil. Give instructions along the following lines.

**On your paper, please write this nursery rhyme:**
**"Jack and Jill went up the hill to fetch a pail of water;**
**Jack fell down and broke his crown and Jill came tumbling after."**

**Now here's your challenge. Change these two phrases in the poem: "fetch a pail of water" and "Jill came tumbling after." The result has to rhyme. The team that most radically alters the meaning of this story by changing those phrases wins. You've got two minutes! Go!**

When teams have made their changes, have them share their masterpieces with the group. If you like, award a prize for the most altered (or the funniest).

Here are examples of what you might hear:

"Jack and Jill went up the hill to wallow in self-pity;
Jack fell down and broke his crown and Jill did sue the city."

"Jack and Jill went up the hill to catch a mess of fishes;
Jack fell down and broke his crown, fulfilling all Jill's wishes."

On the other hand, some teams may have been stymied. Ask all of them: **Was it easy or hard to make these changes? Why?**

**If I'd asked you to change just one word, which one would you have chosen? Why?**

Note that making major changes—in nursery rhymes or in marriage—can be tough. But even small changes can make a big difference. That's what this session is about.

## Identifying Your Needs
*(5-10 minutes)*

Have group members turn to the "Finding Yourself" section in the Participant's Guide.

**Here's a questionnaire to get you thinking about whether you'd like to improve your marriage.** Give people a couple of minutes to fill it out individually. Then give volunteers the chance to share a few of their answers.

1. Before you were married, which of the following did you agree with? Which do you agree with now?
   ___ "You can't change your spouse."
   ___ "Once we're married, he [or she] will change."
   ___ "I'll get used to him [or her]."
   ___ "I wouldn't change a thing."
   ___ "If things don't change, I'll go crazy."

2. When it comes to changing your spouse's behavior, which of the following have you tried? What were the results?
   ___ nagging
   ___ prayer
   ___ an extreme makeover
   ___ counseling
   ___ brain surgery
   ___ recommending a book
   ___ setting a good example
   ___ bribery
   ___ other _____

3. Let's say your spouse has a habit of leaving dirty clothes on the floor. Which of the following describes your most likely response?
   ___ resentful silence
   ___ yelling, "Why don't you stop leaving dirty clothes on the floor?"
   ___ picking up the clothes and being thankful that he or she isn't dead or having an affair
   ___ starting small by asking him or her to pick up just the socks
   ___ declaring a zero tolerance policy on all dirty laundry
   ___ other _____

4. Would you rather lose one pound a week for six months, or a pound a day for a month? Why? _____

5. **Would you rather try to quadruple your savings account in 40 days or 40 years? Why?** _____

6. **What might the two previous questions have to do with the process of improving your marriage?** _____

Most of these are opinion questions, of course, and answers will vary. After hearing replies to the last question, though, you may want to add comments like the following.

**Whether we're talking about losing weight or making money, it's usually easier to make changes slowly and in small steps rather than trying to "build Rome in a day." That's true of marriage, too. In our DVD presentation, Dr. John Trent and Dr. Greg Smalley have some practical things to say about that.**

## 3. CATCHING THE VISION

## Watching and Discussing the DVD
*(20-25 minutes)*

After viewing the DVD, use questions like these to help couples think through what they saw and heard. To save time, you may want to ask the questions directly rather than having group members write answers in their Participant's Guides and share them.

1. **Do small changes or big ones work best when you're trying to do the following? Why?**
   - **turn up the volume on a car radio**
   - **color your hair**
   - **add salt to soup**
   - **be more honest with your spouse**

   (Answers may vary, but the first three of these adjustments generally are best made in small increments so that they aren't overdone. And a spouse who isn't used to being candid could overcompensate by "letting it all out" in the name of honesty, regardless of its effect on his or her mate.)

2. **How was Dr. John Trent's near-accident like some people's approach to married life? How might one or both spouses be "asleep at the wheel"? What kinds of things wake them up?**

   (Some spouses are on "autopilot," paying little attention to the way their relationships may be drifting. Often it takes a crisis—a mate who wants a separation, for instance—to sound the alarm.)

3. **In each of the following cases, what small course corrections might help? What overcorrections might be too much?**
   - **You want your spouse to help more with household chores.**
   - **Your spouse thinks you spend too much time with your parents.**
   - **You read in a book that husbands and wives should pray together daily, and you've never done it once.**
   - **Your spouse says he or she would like "more physical affection."**

   (Small changes could include adding one chore a month for the next three months to a mate's "to do" list; asking that a spouse have lunch with you once a week instead of with his or her mother; starting with *silent* prayer together; agreeing to have a hug and kiss each morning when leaving for work. Overcorrections might include demands that a spouse make "reparations" by taking on all the chores, or being responsible for chores he or she needs time to learn how to do; prohibitions on a spouse spending *any* time with parents; a new rule requiring daily prayer; pressure to double the frequency of sex.)

4. **How did John Trent solve his "pointing problem"? Would you use his pay-a-fine strategy in the following situations? If not, why not? If so, what would the fine be?**
   - **You keep forgetting to empty the cat litter box, leaving your spouse to take care of it.**
   - **Your spouse wants you to talk more.**
   - **Your spouse wants you to talk less.**
   - **You're usually late getting ready when you're supposed to go out for the evening.**

   (John Trent imposed a fine on himself, enforced by his family. Opinions will vary on whether that strategy would work with most marital problems. A spouse who wants to be held accountable might benefit; using a penalty to get a spouse to talk less or more, however, probably wouldn't address the real issues behind a lack or excess of communication.)

5. **Why did John Trent and his wife pay a babysitter and go to the food court once a week? Would that be a 2-degree change for you, a 45-degree change, or a 180-degree change? What might make a change like that worth it?**
(The Trents needed time together. Answers to the other questions will vary; some couples may be willing to pay anything to get out of the house, while others may lack the resources to pay a sitter. This may be an opportunity for your group to consider trading child-care services.)

6. **How is trying to get your spouse to change like pushing a rope? Which of the following do you think John Trent means when he suggests walking in the right direction while holding on to the rope?**
    • **being a good example to your spouse and encouraging any progress**
    • **telling your spouse where to go and controlling him or her**
    • **staying in step together and keeping your spouse close**
    • **other** _____
(The will to change comes from within. When a spouse is ready to change, he or she needs encouragement and a model [the first and third choices], not commands and controls.)

7. **Have you ever tried to make a change that was "too big"? If so, what happened? Why might one small change lead to another?**
(Group members may recall anything from a home remodeling project to an effort to give up TV for a year. Since a small change is more likely to be successful than a radical one, the positive result can encourage a spouse to try additional changes.)

8. **How would you answer someone who says, "My marriage needs big changes, not small ones"?**
(Opinions will vary; you might point out that a series of slight course corrections can get you closer to your goal than a grand plan that's too demanding to follow.)

## Bible Study
*(10 minutes)*

Depending on the priorities of your group and the time available, have volunteers read some or all of these Bible passages and discuss the questions that follow them.

> *A champion named Goliath, who was from Gath, came out of the Philistine camp. He was over nine feet tall. . . .*
>
> *David said to Saul, "Let no one lose heart on account of this Philistine; your servant will go and fight him."*
>
> *Saul replied, "You are not able to go out against this Philistine and fight him; you are only a boy, and he has been a fighting man from his youth."*
>
> *But David said to Saul . . . "The LORD who delivered me from the paw of the lion and the paw of the bear will deliver me from the hand of this Philistine."*
>
> *Saul said to David, "Go, and the LORD be with you."*
>
> *Then Saul dressed David in his own tunic. He put a coat of armor on him and a bronze helmet on his head. David fastened on his sword over the tunic and tried walking around, because he was not used to them.*
>
> *"I cannot go in these," he said to Saul, "because I am not used to them." So he took them off. Then he took his staff in his hand, chose five smooth stones from the stream, put them in the pouch of his shepherd's bag and, with his sling in his hand, approached the Philistine. . . .*
>
> *As the Philistine moved closer to attack him, David ran quickly toward the battle line to meet him. Reaching into his bag and taking out a stone, he slung it and struck the Philistine on the forehead. The stone sank into his forehead, and he fell facedown on the ground.*
>
> *So David triumphed over the Philistine with a sling and a stone; without a sword in his hand he struck down the Philistine and killed him. (1 Samuel 17:4, 32-34, 37-40, 48-50)*

1. **How did small things make a big difference in this story?**
   (Five stones and a sling did what an army couldn't.)

2. **What did Saul assume about the best way to change the situation? How might that attitude lead to discouragement?**

(Saul probably wanted to fight fire with fire—a champion who was as intimidating as Goliath. When we assume that serious problems require massive resources we don't have, it can convince us to give up.)

3. **What was the real reason for David's success?**

(God's help.)

4. **How could this story serve as a pattern for changing things in a marriage?**

(David's attitude made all the difference. He used what was at hand, including his faith, and took a step in the right direction.)

*When Jesus landed and saw a large crowd, he had compassion on them, because they were like sheep without a shepherd. So he began teaching them many things.*

*By this time it was late in the day, so his disciples came to him. "This is a remote place," they said, "and it's already very late. Send the people away so they can go to the surrounding countryside and villages and buy themselves something to eat."*

*But he answered, "You give them something to eat."*

*They said to him, "That would take eight months of a man's wages! Are we to go and spend that much on bread and give it to them to eat?"*

*"How many loaves do you have?" he asked. "Go and see."*

*When they found out, they said, "Five—and two fish."*

*Then Jesus directed them to have all the people sit down in groups on the green grass. So they sat down in groups of hundreds and fifties. Taking the five loaves and the two fish and looking up to heaven, he gave thanks and broke the loaves. Then he gave them to his disciples to set before the people. He also divided the two fish among them all. They all ate and were satisfied, and the disciples picked up twelve basketfuls of broken pieces of bread and fish. The number of the men who had eaten was five thousand. (Mark 6:34-44)*

5. **How did small things make a big difference in this story?**

(A boy's lunch became a meal for thousands.)

6. **What did the disciples assume about the best way to change the situation?**

(They figured a huge—and unavailable—supply of food was needed.)

7. **What was the real reason why Jesus' approach worked?**
   (The boy gave what he could; divine power did the rest.)

8. **How could this story serve as a pattern for changing things in a marriage?**
   (Instead of assuming we "can't get there from here," we can surrender what we have to God and see what He'll do with it.)

   *He told them another parable: "The kingdom of heaven is like a mustard seed, which a man took and planted in his field. Though it is the smallest of all your seeds, yet when it grows, it is the largest of garden plants and becomes a tree, so that the birds of the air come and perch in its branches."*
   *He told them still another parable: "The kingdom of heaven is like yeast that a woman took and mixed into a large amount of flour until it worked all through the dough." (Matthew 13:31-33)*

9. **Why do you suppose God seems to like using small things in big ways?**
   (It gives us a reason to credit Him instead of the resources He provides; it may be an expression of His creativity or even His sense of humor.)

10. **What's one small thing you think He's used to improve your marriage?**
    (Answers might include a habit or tradition couples have formed, such as praying for each other during the day, leaving love notes on the refrigerator, or sponsoring a needy child in another country. Spouses might also cite a problem that's taught them patience or teamwork, like an illness, financial loss, or personality conflict.)

## Applying the Principles
*(10 minutes)*

Have the group turn to the "Making It Work" section in the Participant's Guide. Allow at least five minutes for people to work through the "flight plan" exercise as couples or individuals.

Then ask volunteers to share what they came up with. Assure the group that no one is required to disclose his or her answers.

If time allows, use questions like the following to discuss the activity.

**Is one course correction in a week enough? Is four too many? Why?**

(Opinions will vary, but most couples probably would find it hard to make more than one significant change in a week.)

**To make these course corrections, what will you need?**

(Possibilities: an attitude adjustment; my spouse's support and cooperation; patience; humility; reliance on God; forgiveness and willingness to forgive; time; reminders when I'm off course.)

**What will the two of you need from God?**

(Answers will vary, but the "fruit of the Spirit" list in Galatians 5:22-23 names several God-given qualities that could help couples change.)

## Reinforcing Your Point
*(5 minutes)*

Encourage group members to read the "Bringing It Home" section of their Participant's Guides later this week. They'll find down-to-earth advice from a counselor on what to do when they want a spouse to change.

You may want to wrap up this session with comments like the following.

**In the weeks ahead we'll be talking about some areas in which you might want your marriage to change. That can be pretty overwhelming, especially if you think everything has to change at once.**

**I hope you'll remember the image of John Trent and the steering wheel. Making adjustments a little at a time works a lot better than making a hard left or right and ending up in the ditch—or giving up and finding yourself headed for the guardrail.**

If possible, encourage any struggling couples to contact a Christian counselor recommended by your church. You may want to print the counselor's contact information and give it to all participants, or even pass out the therapist's business cards.

If your group is comfortable doing so, have a volunteer close the meeting by praying for couples who'll be working on course corrections this week.

# GREAT SEX IN A GODLY MARRIAGE (PART 1)

"America's Family Coaches," Dr. Gary and Barb Rosberg, join forces with author Gary Thomas in this DVD segment to address a subject spouses need to talk about—but often don't.

Gary Thomas reveals that "chemistry" really does play a big part in God's plan for men and women. The Rosbergs share couples' answers to the question, "What do you need to have great sex in a godly marriage?"

## Session Aim

To help spouses understand the differing sexual priorities of men and women, and to be more patient in seeking to meet each other's needs.

## Setting the Stage

- Read this session plan and Chapter 2 in the Participant's Guide.
- Provide pencils or pens.
- If you want to use the Step 1 icebreaker, bring refreshments mentioned in the Song of Solomon—raisins, apples, figs (or Fig Newtons), pomegranates, honey, milk, or grapes.
- Cue up the DVD to segment 2, "Great Sex in a Godly Marriage (Part 1)."

## 1. GETTING TOGETHER

### Optional Icebreaker
*(5 minutes)*

Serving refreshments can help group members relax and get to know each other. In this case, though, you'll accomplish more than that.

Bring one or more of the following foods to your meeting place: raisins, apples, figs (or Fig Newtons), pomegranates, honey, milk, or grapes. Have them available as people arrive.

After participants have had a few minutes to enjoy the food and each other's company, ask: **Can anybody tell me what these foods have in common?**

As needed, explain that they're all mentioned in a book of the Bible—the Song of Solomon.

**They're mentioned as things to enjoy. So is sexuality. If you grew up going to church, did you hear much about the Song of Solomon?** (Probably not.) **Why not?** (Perhaps because the sexual content makes some people uncomfortable.)

**If you're new to the church, have you heard much about this book of the Bible yet?** (Probably not.) **Why do you think that is?** (Again, because some people find it too sensual for the sanctuary.)

**It would be hard to talk about marriage without talking about sexuality. Some couples don't do that very often, and it can damage their relationship. Fortunately, we have some experts to bring up the subject in today's DVD segment—so we can sit back and enjoy the refreshments.**

## 2. FINDING YOURSELF

### Identifying Your Needs
*(5-10 minutes)*

Draw the group's attention to the "Finding Yourself" section in the Participant's Guide. Ask: **What are your attitudes about the role of sex in marriage? Here's a survey to get you thinking about that.**

Let group members complete the survey individually. Then have volunteers share a few of their responses—keeping in mind that many people may prefer not to say much about this topic.

1. **Which of the following did you hear in some form when you were growing up? Do you think hearing that influenced you? Why or why not?**
   ___ "Sex is only for married people."
   ___ "Sex is dirty."
   ___ "God created sex."
   ___ "Sex is only for reproduction."
   ___ "People lose interest in sex after they get married."
   ___ "Men want sex; women want love."

2. **Which of the following do you think is the most important part of a good sexual relationship in marriage? Why?**
   ___ good physical health
   ___ a sense of humor
   ___ trust
   ___ good personal hygiene
   ___ emotional closeness
   ___ physical attraction
   ___ spiritual commitment
   ___ other _____

3. **Which of the following do you think most married couples struggle with?**
   ___ how often to have sex
   ___ being too busy to have a love life
   ___ being too tired or stressed for sex
   ___ infidelity
   ___ pornography
   ___ lack of knowledge about sex
   ___ overcoming past sexual abuse

4. **When was the last time you saw a marital sexual relationship portrayed positively on TV or in a movie? Do you see that often?** _____
   _____

5. **Do you think Christians talk too much about the sexual part of marriage, not enough, or about the right amount? Why?** _____

_____

6. **Do you think most sex education classes do a good job of preparing people for marriage? Why or why not?** _____

_____

Since these are mostly opinion questions, you don't have to deliver the "right" answers. Still, you may want to wrap up this step with comments like the following.

**We might have very different backgrounds when it comes to sexuality. And the differences between men and women guarantee that we don't all see this subject in the same way. Our DVD presentation offers proof of that, and suggests how we can deal with those differences in our marriages.**

## Watching and Discussing the DVD
*(20-25 minutes)*

After viewing the DVD, ask the following questions (which appear in the Participant's Guide) to help group members consider what they saw and heard.

1. **Do you think most couples today know more about sex when they get married than couples 50 years ago did? If so, has it made marriages happier? Do you think today's brides and grooms understand the role of sex in marriage better than in the "olden days"? Why or why not?**
   (Answers will vary, but it's true that information about sex is much more readily available—through the Internet, TV, classes, and other sources—than it was 50 years ago. Some group members may feel this is a good thing, enabling married couples to find greater satisfaction and closeness; others may prefer the relative modesty and lower expectations of the "olden days.")

2. **Do you agree with Gary Thomas that God gave men a sex drive that renews their affection for their wives? Do you think it works as a "glue" in most marriages? Why or why not?**

(Opinions may differ. For married couples with a healthy relationship, sex often does strengthen the bond. For others, sexual activity doesn't repair rifts—and the differences in their approaches to sex may create more distance between them.)

3. **According to Gary Thomas, husbands are likely to feel closer to their wives after sex than they will after a long talk about feelings. If that's true, how could it affect the following aspects of a marriage?**
   - **the frequency of sexual relations**
   - **the husband's interest in conversation**
   - **the wife's interest in sex**
   - **the couple's overall sense of closeness**

(Couples might want sex more frequently if they depend on it to maintain feelings of closeness. A husband's interest in conversation might be less than his interest in sex if the latter leaves him feeling closer to his wife. A wife might be more interested in sex if it helps her husband feel closer to her, but only if it has a similar effect on her. If the relationship is otherwise healthy, the couple's overall sense of closeness might benefit from more frequent sex—up to a point. In any case, Gary Thomas' statement helps to explain why many husbands seem more interested in sex than in conversation.)

4. **Which of the following would you expect a Puritan pastor to say? Why? Which of these statements best reflects the attitude toward sex that you learned growing up?**
   - **"Control yourself."**
   - **"Do not let your conjugal love grow lukewarm."**
   - **"Whatever feeleth good, doest thou it."**
   - **"An idle mind is the devil's playground."**
   - **other** _____

(The first and fourth statements are more stereotypically puritanical. As mentioned in the video, a Puritan pastor did make the second statement—probably to the surprise of some people today. Group members may have been exposed to a wide variety of attitudes about sex as they grew up; to encourage honest discussion, resist the urge to "correct" those attitudes at this point.)

5. Do you think the phrases "great sex" and "godly marriage" belong in the same sentence? Why or why not? Which of the following statements would you agree with? Why?
   - The more godly your marriage is, the greater the sex will be.
   - Truly godly people don't pursue great sex.
   - You can have great sex without being godly.
   - Godliness prevents great sex.

   (Participants may feel pressured to give the "right" answer; assure them that it's okay to question whether spirituality automatically leads to greater sexual satisfaction.)

6. Research by Dr. Gary and Barb Rosberg revealed the following top "sex needs" among husbands. If you're a man, would you rank them in this order? If you had to add two others, what would they be? Why?
   - mutual satisfaction
   - connection
   - responsiveness
   - initiation
   - affirmation

   (Rankings and additions will vary, assuming men are willing to voice them. If the silence is overwhelming, you may want to ask men to rank one of the less "embarrassing" needs, affirmation.)

7. The Rosbergs found the following love-life ingredients most valued among wives. If you're a woman, would you rank them in this order? If you had to add two others, what would they be? Why?
   - affirmation
   - connection
   - non-sexual touch
   - romance
   - spiritual intimacy

   (Again, rankings and additions will vary. If women are reluctant to discuss their needs, you might start with the relatively nonthreatening "romance.")

8. **Why do you suppose "connection" and "affirmation" are the only two items on both lists? How might a husband and wife connect with each other despite their sexual differences? How might they affirm each other despite those differences?**

(Perhaps connection and affirmation are the most basic human needs on the lists. Connecting and affirming despite differences may require understanding your spouse's needs, valuing your spouse for more than what he or she can give you, giving up the idea of turning your spouse into someone else, and trusting God that your own needs will be met.)

## Bible Study
*(10 minutes)*

If Bible study is one of your group's goals, read these passages and discuss the questions that follow them.

> *Marriage should be honored by all, and the marriage bed kept pure, for God will judge the adulterer and all the sexually immoral. (Hebrews 13:4)*

1. **What are three ways in which you can "honor" marriage?**
(Some possibilities: by staying sexually faithful; by not making disparaging jokes about it; by carrying out your wedding vows; by putting your best efforts into maintaining it.)

2. **What does it mean for the marriage bed to be "pure"? What does this imply about how God views sex inside and outside of marriage?**
(Purity here probably refers to the opposite of adultery and sexual immorality—which would be limiting sexual activity to the husband-wife relationship. If God sees that as pure, He must have a positive view of marital sex and a negative one of the extramarital kind.)

*[Lover]*
*I have come into my garden, my sister, my bride;*
    *I have gathered my myrrh with my spice.*
    *I have eaten my honeycomb and my honey;*
    *I have drunk my wine and my milk.*
*[Friends]*
*Eat, O friends, and drink;*
    *drink your fill, O lovers.*
*[Beloved]*
*I slept but my heart was awake.*
    *Listen! My lover is knocking:*
    *"Open to me, my sister, my darling,*
    *my dove, my flawless one.*
    *My head is drenched with dew,*
    *my hair with the dampness of the night." . . .*
*O daughters of Jerusalem, I charge you—*
*if you find my lover,*
*what will you tell him?*
*Tell him I am faint with love.*
*[Friends]*
*How is your beloved better than others,*
    *most beautiful of women?*
    *How is your beloved better than others,*
    *that you charge us so?*
*[Beloved]*
*My lover is radiant and ruddy,*
    *outstanding among ten thousand.*
*His head is purest gold;*
*his hair is wavy*
*and black as a raven.*
*His eyes are like doves*
*by the water streams,*
*washed in milk,*
*mounted like jewels.*
*His cheeks are like beds of spice*

*yielding perfume.*
*His lips are like lilies*
*dripping with myrrh.*
*His arms are rods of gold*
*set with chrysolite.*
*His body is like polished ivory*
*decorated with sapphires.*
*His legs are pillars of marble*
*set on bases of pure gold.*
*His appearance is like Lebanon,*
*choice as its cedars.*
*His mouth is sweetness itself;*
*he is altogether lovely.*
*This is my lover, this my friend,*
*O daughters of Jerusalem. (Song of Songs 5:1-2, 8-16)*

3. **Why do you suppose passages like this are in the Bible?**
   (Some believe the Song of Solomon (or Songs) is primarily a symbolic description of the spiritual relationship between God and His people. Others say the book affirms God's approval of the physical, sensual relationship between husband and wife, which He invented.)

4. **How would you change the beloved's descriptions of her lover's head, hair, eyes, cheeks, lips, arms, body, legs, appearance, and mouth to fit our culture and time?**
   (It's hard for most of us to get excited about eyes that are "washed in milk." Updating the nature-oriented descriptions for our day might involve comparisons to movie stars, food, cars, and electronic devices. Let the group have some fun with this if time allows.)

5. **If you wrote a note like this to your spouse, what do you think would be his or her reaction?**
   (Group members might predict anything from laughter to shock to appreciation to writing a similar note in return.)

## Applying the Principles
*(10 minutes)*

Invite the group to turn to the "Making It Work" section in the Participant's Guide. Let people complete the "surprise package" exercise, working individually. Then give couples a few minutes to get each other's reactions to their rankings of the presents.

If time allows, discuss the activity as a group—using questions like the following.

**Some people say about gift-giving, "It's the thought that counts." Is that true in this case? Why or why not?**

(Opinions may differ. The thought is important, but unless the recipient's need is truly met, the giver would do well to think harder about the recipient's point of view.)

**When you compared your spouse's rankings with your own, what did you learn about your spouse? What did you learn about yourself?**

(Participants may not want to talk about issues like initiation and responsiveness, but with your encouragement might discuss their differences in more general terms. For example, a wife might be surprised to learn that her husband was more interested in romance than she thought he was. In any case, avoid pressing anyone for an answer.)

**Some of the presents may seem a little abstract. What might be in the boxes containing spiritual intimacy and romance?**

(Listen to the group's ideas. As needed, add that spiritual intimacy might include talking honestly about a doubt or prayer request, listening to a praise song together, sharing hopes for your children's spiritual growth, or wondering together about what heaven will be like. Romance could involve dim lights and soft music, but might also take the form of publicly declaring your love or your spouse's desirability and character.)

**Is it better to give something that your spouse really wants but you don't care strongly about, or something you think truly expresses your love but your spouse could easily live without? Why?**

(Perspectives will vary. In terms of meeting needs, the former choice probably is better. If you can help your spouse understand the "why" of your gift, he or she will appreciate it more. Until then, it might be best to give both gifts.)

**This week, when you give your spouse one of these gifts, what will you do if the response isn't quite what you hoped for?**

(Answers will differ. You may want to remind couples that reacting with forgiveness and patience will go a long way toward providing two of the "most wanted" items on the lists of both men and women: affirmation and connection.)

## Reinforcing Your Point
*(5 minutes)*

Draw couples' attention to the "Bringing It Home" section of their Participants' Guides. Encourage them to read later the therapist's advice on what to do when husband and wife aren't on the same page, sexually speaking.

To conclude this session, try comments like the following.

**If you haven't read much of the Song of Solomon, maybe you're a little more interested now. Your spouse's legs may look more like pretzel sticks than pillars of marble, but we can learn a lot from that book. It celebrates the kind of relationship God meant husbands and wives to enjoy.**

**Next time we'll talk about some everyday problems couples have with their love lives. I guarantee we won't solve all of them. But at least we'll be talking about them with God's perspective in mind. And that's a start.**

If you like, close by thanking God for His gift of physical intimacy in marriage. Ask Him to help those who are giving and receiving the "gifts" discussed in this session to do so in a way that brings glory to Him.

# GREAT SEX IN A GODLY MARRIAGE (PART 2)

Ready for some straight talk from authors Kay Arthur and Dr. Juli Slattery?

In this DVD segment, Kay challenges us to take a biblical view of God's good gift of sexuality, swimming against the cultural current that excuses infidelity and short-term wedlock. Juli, a psychologist, is frank and funny as she tackles the question of how real couples—even parents of little kids—can have sex lives. How can you find time to be intimate? What if you don't feel attractive? How can you get your spouse more interested in sex?

If you sometimes find physical intimacy to be more of a minefield than a mountaintop experience, this session is for you.

## Session Aim

To help couples guard their sex lives against two common threats—infidelity and apathy.

## Setting the Stage

- Read this session plan and Chapter 2 in the Participant's Guide.
- Provide pencils or pens.
- If you want to use the Step 1 icebreaker activity, bring two bridal magazines (or any two magazines related to marriage). You may want to bring prizes for the duelists, too.
- Cue up the DVD to segment 3, "Great Sex in a Godly Marriage (Part 2)."

### Optional Icebreaker
*(5 minutes)*

Bring two bridal magazines (or any two magazines related to marriage). Form two teams; each team picks a champion.

Roll up the magazines and give one to each of the champions. Announce that the champions are going to have a duel. They must stand at least four feet apart at all times; the first to knock the magazine out of the other's hand wins. Duelists may not strike each other; only the rolled-up reading materials may touch.

Encourage teams to cheer on their champions. Allow up to 90 seconds for the duel. If neither contestant wins during that time, declare a tie. Award a prize to each duelist if you wish.

After thanking your champions, say something like the following.

**Do you think these magazines were appropriate weapons? Why or why not?**

**These publications were meant to bring people together. Instead, they kept our duelists apart. Sometimes the sexual part of marriage is that way. In this session we're going to talk about what to do with sexuality in a world that can't seem to understand what it's for.**

### Identifying Your Needs
*(5-10 minutes)*

Have people turn to the "Finding Yourself" section in the Participant's Guide. Say: **It's time to express some opinions. Here's a survey about some attitudes you may be bringing to this meeting.**

Let group members complete the questionnaire individually. Then let volunteers share a few of their responses—keeping in mind that many people may prefer not to say much about this topic.

1.  **If you needed advice about sex, where would you go? Why?**
    ___ the Internet
    ___ a marriage counselor
    ___ a sex therapist
    ___ a pastor
    ___ a book
    ___ other _____

    (If people would rather not answer this aloud, encourage them to whisper the answer to their spouses.)

2.  **Which of the following is most like your love life these days?**
    ___ The Discovery Channel
    ___ The History Channel
    ___ MTV
    ___ Comedy Central
    ___ other _____

    (The chances of getting serious answers to this question are slim, but rest assured that participants will be thinking about it.)

3.  **Which of the following do you think would result in the biggest improvement in most married people's sexual lives?**
    ___ if men were more like women
    ___ if women were more like men
    ___ if everybody became a Christian
    ___ if the electricity went off after 9:00 P.M. every night
    ___ if pornographers went out of business
    ___ if everyone joined a health club
    ___ other _____

    (Answers may vary widely; ask group members to explain their replies, but don't challenge them at this point.)

4.  **In 25 words or less, how would you summarize what the Bible says about sexuality?** _____
    _____

(Many answers are possible. Reinforce key points participants mention, such as the fact that God created sexuality, that sex outside marriage is off limits, and that marital sex is meant for enjoyment as well as procreation.)

5.  **Do you think the way to a man's heart is through his stomach? Why or why not? What do you think is the way to a woman's heart?** _____

_____

(There's no "right" answer to these questions; the important thing is to get people thinking about possible connections between emotional and physical intimacy.)

6.  **Do you think those with a strong faith have better sexual relationships in their marriages than others do? Why or why not?** _____

_____

(Some participants may feel they must say yes out of loyalty to their faith, no matter what they really think. Others may be reluctant to speculate, since they have no evidence either way. As needed, point out that some research has indicated that couples with a strong faith report a higher level of satisfaction with their sex lives than other couples do. This doesn't mean, of course, that all devout couples experience that.)

## Watching and Discussing the DVD
*(20-25 minutes)*

After viewing the DVD, use questions like these to help group members think through what they saw and heard.

1.  **Which of the following comes closest to describing your response to this DVD segment? Why?**
    - **Let's move on to a less embarrassing subject.**
    - **It gave me a lot to think about.**
    - **It needed more guys.**

- **It gave me hope.**
- **other** _____

(Answers will vary; avoid favoring one reaction over another.)

2. **Does it matter to you what the "biblical view of sexuality" is? If so, could you prove in court how much it matters to you? Why or why not?**
(If some group members express doubt about the importance of a biblical view or question whether the views expressed in the DVD presentation are biblical, keep in mind that you've asked for a personal opinion. Encourage these participants to keep watching and listening as they make up their minds. For others, point out that legal evidence would include actions and statements. Since most group members probably haven't made many public declarations on the subject, actions will speak louder than words. Faithfulness in marriage and an effort to learn more about the biblical view of sexuality might be submitted as evidence.)

3. **How would you describe Kay Arthur's approach to sexuality? How do you think the following people would describe it? Why?**
   - **the characters on TV shows like *Friends* and *Two and a Half Men***
   - **Christians of the past like Martin Luther and John Bunyan**
   - **contemporary Christians in Africa**
   - **American Christians 20 years from now**
(Some may find Kay's approach outmoded; others may feel it's timeless. Many TV characters might describe it as quaint, laughable, or puritanical; Martin Luther and John Bunyan probably would have agreed with much of it, though they might have been shocked to see a woman speaking publicly on this topic. Some African Christians might wonder about references to appearance or the role of a wife; if present cultural trends continue, future American believers might claim Kay's view is too restrictive.)

4. **Kay points out that God designed sex, that it's good and beautiful and bonds spouses together. How could you try to convince the following people of that fact?**
   - **a husband who grew up hearing in church that sex is dirty**
   - **a wife who was sexually abused as a child**

- **a husband who believes sex is just a matter of hormones and instinct**
- **a wife who finds sex boring and unfulfilling**

(Suggestions will vary. Since most of what we know about God and His view comes from the Bible, presenting a convincing case might depend on the person's view of Scripture. For some people, knowing a Christian with a healthy attitude toward sexuality would help.)

5. **Dr. Juli Slattery notes that in one survey more than 80 percent of husbands said their fondest desire was that their wives would initiate sex more often. Does this surprise you? Why or why not?**

(Reactions will vary. This desire of husbands has been expressed in books and other media, though group members may be surprised that it's number one for so many.)

6. **According to Juli, a wife wants to know that her husband doesn't just want to have sex, but wants to have sex with her. How can a husband make this clear to his wife?**

(Perhaps by paying attention to her inside and outside the bedroom, making eye contact, not ogling women who pass by or appear on TV, and saying and doing things that prove he knows her well and cherishes her unique qualities.)

7. **Juli points out the importance of telling your spouse about your need for physical intimacy. What do you think is the best time of day to do this? The best place? Why?**

(As needed, suggest that sensitive topics should be discussed when both spouses are relatively relaxed, rested, and have time to talk, in a place that's private and uninterrupted by children or electronic devices.)

## 4. DIGGING DEEPER

### Bible Study
*(10 minutes)*

If your group makes Bible study a priority, read some or all of these passages and discuss the questions that follow them.

*"Everything is permissible for me"—but not everything is beneficial. "Everything is permissible for me"—but I will not be mastered by anything. "Food for the stomach and the stomach for food"—but God will destroy them both. The body is not meant for sexual immorality, but for the Lord, and the Lord for the body. By his power God raised the Lord from the dead, and he will raise us also. Do you not know that your bodies are members of Christ himself? Shall I then take the members of Christ and unite them with a prostitute? Never! Do you not know that he who unites himself with a prostitute is one with her in body? For it is said, "The two will become one flesh." But he who unites himself with the Lord is one with him in spirit.*

*Flee from sexual immorality. All other sins a man commits are outside his body, but he who sins sexually sins against his own body. Do you not know that your body is a temple of the Holy Spirit, who is in you, whom you have received from God? You are not your own; you were bought at a price. Therefore honor God with your body. (1 Corinthians 6:12-20)*

1. **If sexuality is God-given, good, and beautiful, why are all these warnings necessary?**
(Sexuality is also powerful and easily misused. The church in Corinth had problems in this area, and Paul's instructions were aimed at them as well as benefiting Christians in general.)

2. **Which verse in 1 Corinthians 6:12-20 do you think would be most controversial in our society today? Why?**
(Many would reject the idea that Christ rose from the dead; some would be offended that the passage seems "disrespectful" to prostitutes; the statement that we don't belong to ourselves would be widely dismissed. But the notion that certain sexual behavior is "immoral" and "sin" and that we should run from it might be the most disturbing to our society.)

*Now for the matters you wrote about: It is good for a man not to marry. But since there is so much immorality, each man should have his own wife, and each woman her own husband. The husband should fulfill his marital duty to his wife, and likewise the wife to her husband. The wife's body does not belong to her alone but also to her husband. In the same way, the husband's body does not belong to him alone but also to his wife. Do not deprive each other except by mutual consent and for a time, so that you may devote yourselves to prayer. Then come together again so that Satan will not tempt you because of your lack of self-control. I say this as a concession, not as a command. I wish that all men were as I am. But each man has his own gift from God; one has this gift, another has that. (1 Corinthians 7:1-7)*

3. **If marriage is God-given, good, and beautiful, why did Paul say it was good to stay single?**
   (Perhaps he was saying it was permissible; perhaps he meant that there were some advantages to not being married, such as the ability to devote more time and energy to service. The fact that marriage is good doesn't mean singleness is bad, and vice versa.)

4. **Does "marital duty" refer only to sex? Does it imply that sex is a chore? Why or why not?**
   (Since the passage refers to the bodies of wife and husband, it would seem to be mainly about sex. But when the Bible's whole counsel on marriage is considered, it seems clear that the "duties" of spouses include things like love and respect. The word "duty" often is associated with drudgery in our culture, but it can also be seen as an honorable obligation.)

5. **Which verse in 1 Corinthians 7:1-7 do you think would be most controversial in our society today? Why?**
   (Some might think Paul's endorsement of marriage is halfhearted and unromantic. Many would think it inhuman and even sick to give up sex temporarily in order to devote oneself to prayer.)

   *If a man has recently married, he must not be sent to war or have any other duty laid on him. For one year he is to be free to stay at home and bring happiness to the wife he has married. (Deuteronomy 24:5)*

6. **Why do you suppose this rule was included in the Bible? What does it tell you about God's attitude toward the pleasurable aspects of marriage?**
   (God must put a high priority on marriage, and knows that it has great potential to bring couples happiness. In fact, He must want them to seek that kind of happiness, not just grit their teeth and honor their vows.)

7. **Does a husband's responsibility to bring his wife happiness end after the first year? How do you know? Does this apply to the wife as well? Why or why not?**

(Husbands are urged to love their wives indefinitely, both sexually and as Christ loves the church [Proverbs 5:18-19; Ephesians 5:25-33]. Proverbs 5:19 also expresses the wish that a husband will "ever be captivated by [his wife's] love." This would seem to imply some effort on her part, too.)

## 5. MAKING IT WORK

### Applying the Principles
*(10 minutes)*

Have people turn to the "Making It Work" section in the Participant's Guide. Let them complete the exercise, working individually. Then give spouses a few minutes to talk over their answers.

Many couples probably will prefer not to share their conclusions with the whole group. So wrap up the discussion by having only spouses address questions like the following with each other.

**Which of the suggestions for wives made the most sense to you? Why?**

(Answers will vary. Encourage couples to spend this time talking about the ideas they'd like to use rather than criticizing the ones they wouldn't.)

**Which of the suggestions for husbands did you find most valuable? Why?**

(Again, couples should pick the best and ignore the rest for now.)

**Which of the items on the "obstacles" lists could your spouse help you with? Which would you most like help with this week?**

(Answers will vary, but in general spouses may be most qualified to help by offering reassurance. For example, a husband might affirm that his wife is still attractive, or that the two of them can afford it if she wants to buy a new outfit. A wife might assure her husband that she won't reject him if he offers her a back rub, or that she'll believe him if he says having sex with her is important to him. If schedules are a problem, spouses may be able to help by spending less time on a hobby and setting aside time for intimacy.)

If you think spouses will be comfortable doing so, ask them to pray together about the obstacles they circled. Encourage them to follow through this week on the easier of the two suggestions they chose.

## 6. BRINGING IT HOME

### Reinforcing Your Point
*(5 minutes)*

Draw couples' attention to the "Bringing It Home" section of their Participants' Guides. Encourage them to read later the therapist's advice on how spouses can build—or rebuild—a sexual relationship.

**As this counselor points out, the success of your love life isn't just about technique. A lot of it has to do with what goes on outside the bedroom.**

**So even though this wraps up our two sessions on sexuality, it's a subject that ties into others we'll be talking about. For instance, next time we'll look at anger. If you think anger can't affect your love life, or that your love life can't make you angry, you probably haven't been married more than five minutes or so. Or your marriage is perfect, and you'll be leading the group next time.**

Close by asking God to bless the relationships represented in the room. Ask Him to help couples overcome the obstacles they identified earlier.

Session 4

# EXPRESSING YOUR ANGER THE RIGHT WAY

Is it possible to have marriage without anger? Yes, if both spouses are robots!

For the rest of us, this DVD segment examines how anger affects *human* couples—and how they can keep it from eating away at their relationship. Family coaches Dr. Gary and Barb Rosberg team up with psychologist and educator Dr. Archibald Hart to explain how to keep this powerful emotion from turning into rage or revenge. Host Dr. Greg Smalley shares a down-to-earth story on the subject, too.

Every marriage has anger; find out how to manage it instead of letting it manage you.

## Session Aim

To help spouses express their anger in ways that bring them together instead of driving them apart.

## Setting the Stage

- Read this session plan and Chapter 4 in the Participant's Guide.
- Provide pencils or pens.
- Make photocopies of "The Vicious Circle Game" in Step 1 (one copy per couple) if you plan to use it, and bring two pennies for each couple.
- Cue up the DVD to segment 4, "Expressing Your Anger the Right Way."

## 1. GETTING TOGETHER

### Optional Icebreaker
*(5 minutes)*

This opening activity may leave group members feeling slightly steamed—but that should get them ready for this session's topic.

Before the session, photocopy the following "board game." Make a copy for each couple. Bring two pennies for each couple, too.

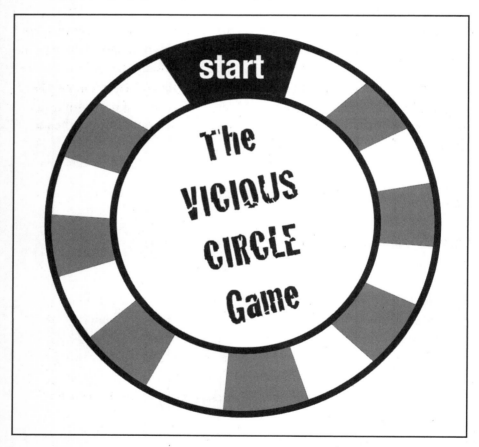

After handing out the game boards and pennies, give instructions like the following.

**Let's start with a really fun game. It's "The Vicious Circle Game," and here's how to play.**

Use your penny as a game piece. Start anywhere on the circle. Take turns, moving one space at a time. No matter what space you land on, tell your spouse one of your pet peeves—something that drives you crazy. The object is to name as many pet peeves as possible. We'll do this for two minutes. Go!

Let couples play the game for two minutes. Then discuss briefly what happened.

**Wasn't this a fun game? Couldn't you play it for hours?** (Probably not.)

**Do you feel better or worse than before you started playing?** (Some may benefit from having "let off steam," but others may find that griping about irritants just made them more irritated.)

**How is this game like some people's marriages?** (They find lots of things to get angry about; they just go around in circles, never making progress in solving the problems that make them angry; nobody wins.)

**Anger is part of practically every marriage. Unfortunately, it's not a game. Anger isn't good or bad in itself, but the way we express and deal with it can make the difference between a great relationship and a "vicious circle" we'd like to escape.**

## Identifying Your Needs
*(5-10 minutes)*

Have people turn to the "Finding Yourself" section in the Participant's Guide.

**Here's a survey; please take a few minutes to fill it out.** Have group members do this individually. Then let volunteers share some answers with the whole group.

1. **In your opinion, which of the following words describe anger? Why?**
   \_\_\_ **dangerous**
   \_\_\_ **cleansing**
   \_\_\_ **sinful**
   \_\_\_ **righteous**
   \_\_\_ **normal**
   \_\_\_ **exhausting**

(Anger could be any of these things, depending on the circumstances. The important thing is to get group members thinking about whether they tend to label all or most anger as good, bad, or otherwise.)

2.  **Which of the following do you think Jesus might say about anger? Why?**
    ____ **"You have heard it said that fighting is evil; I tell you that anyone who grows angry will not inherit the kingdom of heaven."**
    ____ **"Blessed are those who are angry for My sake."**
    ____ **"The anger of man is of no consequence to God."**
    ____ **"Be angry as I am angry."**
    ____ **"If you are angry at another, you are angry at Me."**

(The Bible doesn't record that Jesus made any of these statements. He didn't condemn anger itself, nor did He commend getting mad on His behalf. Scripture does say that God isn't impressed with many human activities, but not that He dismisses our emotions. Jesus was angry in some situations [Matthew 21:12-13], but didn't specifically call His followers to anger. He said that holding a grudge interferes with our ability to worship Him, but didn't say that being angry at another person is always wrong.)

3.  **Rank the following in order to show how angry you think each situation would make your spouse—from most to least upset.**
    ____ **You ate a piece of the cake your spouse was saving for a party at work.**
    ____ **You accidentally sat on your spouse's eyeglasses and broke them.**
    ____ **You forgot to pay the electric bill, and the power to your home has been shut off.**
    ____ **You made a joke about your spouse's weight in front of friends.**
    ____ **You're having an affair.**
    ____ **You're 30 minutes late getting ready for church.**

(If participants are reluctant to share answers because they fear it might embarrass their mates, that's fine. Simply thinking about the situations is enough, since the point is to help people consider their spouses' anger "triggers.")

4.  **If anger were furniture, what would your living room look like? Would it be crowded? Would the furniture be old or new?** _____
    _____

(Your goal here is to get couples thinking about the amount of anger in their marriage. Would their living rooms look like a garage sale or antique store, piled high with grudges? Understandably, some couples may not want to answer this aloud. You may want to be ready with an answer of your own.)

5. **If you had to rewrite your wedding vows to include a statement about anger, what would it be?** _____

_____

(Answers will vary, based on what each participant has learned about anger since the wedding day. Examples: "In sickness and in health, for richer, for poorer, in irritation and in rage . . ." or "We promise not to speak to each other at a volume louder than our kitchen blender.")

6. **Is there any way in which anger could help a marriage? If so, what might it be? If not, why not?** _____

_____

(Anger can help spotlight a marital problem, making its resolution a higher priority. If both spouses are angry at an injustice done to a third party, doing something about it together can be a bonding experience. Some might say that anger, if followed by forgiveness and "making up," can bring a couple closer—though counting on anger to accomplish that could lead to chronic conflict.)

## 3. CATCHING THE VISION

### Watching and Discussing the DVD
*(20-25 minutes)*

After viewing the DVD, discuss questions like these from the Participant's Guide. Due to their personal nature, you might want spouses to address questions 1, 5, 6, and 7 only with each other.

1. **If you and your spouse were guests on a TV psychologist's show, which of the following might be the title of that episode? Why?**
   - **"Spouses Who Throw Things, and the Dishes They've Broken"**
   - **"Spouses Who Argue, and the Pets Who Avoid Them"**

- **"Spouses Who Clam Up, and the Silence That's Deafening"**
- **other** _____

(Answers will vary, as will participants' desire to reply aloud.)

2. **Dr. Gary and Barb Rosberg say they've met many Christians who don't think anger is a God-given emotion. What might these people believe instead?**
(That God-given emotions are all "positive," and that anger is the opposite; that anger represents a refusal to accept God's will; that anger is always selfish.)

3. **How could anger play a positive role in each of the following situations?**
- **During an argument, your spouse blurts out that your spending on clothes is higher than the mortgage payment.**
- **You and your spouse get mad when you learn that a neighbor is endangering her children by using a kerosene heater in her house.**
- **Your spouse threatens to call the doctor if you don't start taking your blood pressure medication regularly.**
- **When your spouse refuses to see a marriage counselor with you, you're so angry you decide to see a counselor on your own.**

(In all these situations, anger could lead to constructive action.)

4. **The Rosbergs note that spouses may get angry when they're criticized. Why are the following not good ways to deal with that? Why? What would be a better strategy?**
- **Never criticize your spouse.**
- **Deliver all your criticism in the form of anonymous letters.**
- **Preface your criticism with, "I know you think you're perfect, but . . ."**
- **When your spouse reacts angrily, say, "I knew you'd do that."**

(These responses either require "walking on eggs" around your spouse, afraid to "set him [or her] off," or are ways to indirectly attack your spouse. The first approach requires the "egg-walker" to suppress anger instead of dealing with it, making it more likely to emerge later in a more destructive form. The second approach prolongs the criticism, conflict, and anger.)

5. Dr. Archibald Hart has said that anger is like a smoke alarm; it tells you that something's wrong and you need to figure out what it is. In your home, what kinds of things tend to set off the alarm?
   - annoying habits
   - lack of communication
   - conflict over money, chores, in-laws, or sex
   - differences in parenting
   - other _____

(Unless your group is unusually forthcoming, let spouses reply only to each other.)

6. What's your usual response when the "smoke alarm" of anger goes off in your home? How do you feel about that?
   - I panic and call the "fire department."
   - I take out the "battery" to make the noise stop.
   - I make sure everybody is safe and look for the source of the smoke.
   - other _____

(If participants are willing to answer, ask them to explain what "fire department" and "battery" mean to them, and how they look for the smoke's source.)

7. Dr. Hart suggests several steps to take when you feel angry with your spouse. Which of these are hardest for you? Why?
   - Acknowledge that you feel angry and reflect on that.
   - Gain control of yourself.
   - Take a "time out" if necessary to slow things down.
   - Take responsibility for your feelings.
   - If you said something inappropriate, apologize immediately.

(If people want to discuss this only with their spouses, don't press them to do otherwise. If they're willing to share with the group, though, it might encourage others to know they aren't the only ones who struggle with this.)

8. According to Dr. Hart, forgiveness is the best antidote to anger. What happens if you refuse to give that antidote to your spouse?
   (It poisons your relationship.)

## 4. DIGGING DEEPER

### Bible Study
*(10 minutes)*

The Bible has a lot to say about anger. Here are several passages your group can, if you wish, apply to anger in marriage.

> *A fool shows his annoyance at once, but a prudent man overlooks an insult. . . .*
> *A fool gives full vent to his anger, but a wise man keeps himself under control.*
> *(Proverbs 12:16; 29:11)*

1. **What do you conclude about anger from these proverbs?**
   ____ **It's a sin.**
   ____ **It's powerful.**
   ____ **You should resist it.**
   ____ **You should resist expressing it.**
   ____ **other** _____

(These proverbs may imply that anger is powerful, but not that it's wrong. They might be paraphrased as "Don't fly off the handle." If resisting the expression of anger means thinking twice before reacting, then resisting is good; if it means suppressing feelings that may explode later, it's not.)

> *For as churning the milk produces butter, and as twisting the nose produces*
> *blood, so stirring up anger produces strife. (Proverbs 30:33)*

2. **Have you ever stirred up anger in your marriage by doing one of the following things? Would you recommend that to other couples? Why or why not?**
   ____ **bringing up an old conflict that hasn't been resolved**
   ____ **criticizing your in-laws**
   ____ **asking why your spouse isn't more like your mother or father**
   ____ **breaking a promise**
   ____ **teasing your spouse about a subject you know is "sensitive"**

(If group members are reluctant to answer the "confessional" part of the question, concentrate on the "recommendation" part. Have an example of your own ready if possible.)

*"In your anger do not sin": Do not let the sun go down while you are still angry. (Ephesians 4:26)*

3. **When does anger become sin? How does dealing with anger quickly keep it from turning into sin? What usually happens if you and your spouse don't address anger within 24 hours?**

(It's not that anger becomes sin; it's that when you're angry, there's an opportunity and tendency to do the wrong thing with your anger—such as abusing a spouse, using the Lord's name in vain, getting revenge, or refusing to forgive. The sooner anger is defused, the more likely you'll be able to exercise self-control in the way you respond. You may want to be ready to answer the last part of this question yourself to get the conversation going.)

*For man's anger does not bring about the righteous life that God desires.* (James 1:20)

4. **Which of the following do you think are examples of James 1:20 in action? Why?**
   ____ **A wife threatens to leave her husband unless he goes with her to a marriage counselor.**
   ____ **A husband demands that his wife follow his "spiritual leadership."**
   ____ **A husband shoves his wife during an argument.**
   ____ **A wife discovers pornography on her husband's computer and throws the machine in the garbage.**
   ____ **other** _____

(These could all be examples. As needed, point out that our "righteous indignation" isn't always so righteous. It can help to be accountable to someone else who can help us see the causes of our anger more objectively.)

*[Love] is not rude, it is not self-seeking, it is not easily angered, it keeps no record of wrongs. (1 Corinthians 13:5)*

5. **What does rudeness have to do with anger? What's the difference between getting angry and being easily angered? In a marriage, how does anger often lead to keeping a record of wrongs—and vice versa? How could not keeping such a record reduce the level of anger in a marriage?**

(A spouse's anger can lead to rudeness, and some spouses use anger as an excuse for being rude. Nearly everyone gets angry, just as nearly everyone gets sad or fearful. Being "easily angered" is overreacting or being on the lookout for things to be mad about. An angry spouse often searches for evidence that his or her anger is justified, leading to keeping track of slights real and imagined. Keeping that record only increases the anger, which completes the "vicious circle." Not counting your spouse's shortcomings would help you avoid concentrating on them, giving you the freedom to count your blessings as well.)

## Applying the Principles
*(10 minutes)*

Ask group members to look at the "Making It Work" section in the Participant's Guide. Have them work individually on the "symptoms of anger" diagrams.

Then give couples a few minutes to show each other how they've marked their diagrams, and to discuss their accuracy. Spouses should come up with signals to use during a disagreement when they feel anger symptoms or notice them in each other.

Finally, open the discussion to the group as a whole. Here are some questions you might use.

**Which was harder: describing your own anger symptoms or those of your spouse? Why?**

(Answers will differ; some people are less "in touch with" their own physical and emotional reactions to stress than others are; some spouses may become *less* expressive when they're angry, which makes them difficult to "read.")

**What are some signals you think wouldn't work?**

(You may hear some amusing replies, like "hosing him off with the fire extinguisher," or "saying, 'Don't go away mad, just go away.'" Signals that use humor might help to reduce tension, but only if the confrontation isn't too intense. The best signal may simply be one that both spouses agree on.)

**If you're in the middle of a heated conversation with your spouse and you get "the signal," what would be a healthy response?**

(Acknowledging the signal; taking a "time-out"; thanking the other person for noticing how you were feeling; agreeing to continue the conversation at a specific time in the near future.)

**How long should spouses let each other "cool down" before trying again to discuss a hot topic?**

(Some may suggest that spouses should try again before the day ends [Ephesians 4:26]. The key may be to resume the discussion as soon as both spouses are under control and don't feel rushed. It's unlikely that there will ever be a perfect time, though, so couples may not be able to put off talking until all traces of tension have vanished.)

## 6. BRINGING IT HOME

### Reinforcing Your Point
*(5 minutes)*

Remind group members that the "Bringing It Home" section of their Participant's Guides includes further advice from a licensed counselor—this time on the subject of angry arguments. Encourage them to read it later this week.

To wrap up this session, you might say something like the following.

**Some of you came up with a signal to tell your spouse when it's time to take a break because of anger. If you remember what it is, raise your hand.**

**I hope you still remember it next time you find yourself feeling angry or facing an angry spouse. Maybe you should practice your signal on the way home.**

**When we think about anger, we usually think of energy and intensity. Next time we'll talk about another emotional state that almost seems like the opposite. It's depression. Just like anger, it can affect every aspect of your marriage. You might be surprised at some of the people who've gone through it; we'll hear from three of them and find out how to deal with it.**

If possible, ask a group member to close by praying for couples whose relationships have been strained by anger. You may want to urge spouses who struggle with this problem to contact a counselor recommended by your church.

# DEALING WITH DEPRESSION TOGETHER

You won't find any ivory-tower platitudes in this DVD segment. Three counselors—Mitch Temple, Dr. Gary Rosberg, and Dr. Juli Slattery—tell the unvarnished truth about their own battles with depression.

Any spouse can be hit with a job loss, the death of a loved one, a chemical imbalance, postpartum stress, or other circumstance that spirals downward into hopelessness. What if it's you? What if it's your husband or wife?

Depression can destroy a relationship. In this session, the experts explain what helped them—and their marriages—survive.

## Session Aim

To help group members identify signs of depression in a spouse if such signs exist, to help them urge a depressed spouse to get professional counseling, or to help them prepare for the possibility that they or a spouse will become depressed in the future.

## Setting the Stage

- Read this session plan and Chapter 5 in the Participant's Guide.
- Provide pencils or pens.
- If you want to use the Step 1 icebreaker, draw the "smiley" and "sad" faces on paper plates (one per person) per the instructions in Step 1. You'll also need a recorded song and a way to play it. Bring a prize for the winner(s) of the game if you like.
- Cue up the DVD to segment 5, "Dealing with Depression Together."

## Optional Icebreaker
*(5 minutes)*

Before the session, get enough paper plates so that each group member can have one. Use a marker to draw a simple "smiley" face on all of them except one; that one should have a "sad" face (see the diagrams if you're artistically challenged).

To start your session, have group members sit in a circle. Explain that you're about to play a new version of "Musical Chairs."

Give each person one of the paper plates. **I'm going to start the music. When I do, pass your "face" to the person on your right. Keep passing until I stop the music. Whoever's left with the sad face is out of the game. We'll keep doing this until three minutes are up, or until only one person is left. That person will be the winner.**

Start the music. Let it play for a while, making sure people keep the plates moving. Then stop the music and have the person stuck with the sad face stand in a corner. Give the sad face to a remaining player and take his or her smiley one.

Repeat the process for three minutes or until one person is left. Award a prize to the winner(s) if you want to. Then say something like the following.

**Does our society tend to reward smiley faces or sad ones? If so, how?**

(Happy-looking people are generally regarded as more appealing; we're urged to smile, have a positive viewpoint, and look on the bright side. People who don't smile are called sour, negative, pessimistic, or mean. "Making a good impression" by smiling often leads to success in business, romance, and making friends.)

**If you're really feeling sad, is it better to let it show or to "paste" on a smiley face? Why?**

(Pasting on a smile may keep other people from avoiding you or asking uncomfortable questions, but it doesn't deal with the source of your sadness.)

**If one partner in a marriage is sad most of the time, how might it affect that relationship?**

(The sad spouse may lose interest in activities the couple previously enjoyed, including conversation and sex; the other person may be angry over the sad spouse's inability to "get over it.")

**Society may be satisfied if we just paste on a smile. But marriage requires more honesty than that. When sadness lasts, it may be depression—and it can turn a relationship upside-down.**

## 2. FINDING YOURSELF

### Identifying Your Needs
*(5-10 minutes)*

Ask group members to turn to the "Finding Yourself" section in the Participant's Guide.

**Here are some questions to help you start thinking about the topic of this session.** Allow a couple of minutes for people to complete the questionnaire. Then let volunteers share answers with the whole group.

1. **Which of the following words or phrases come to mind when you hear the word *depression*? Why?**
    _____ **sad**
    _____ **weak**
    _____ **stock market crash**
    _____ **darkness**
    _____ **dent**
    _____ **other** _____

(Since you've already mentioned depression as an emotional state, most people probably will think of "sad" and "darkness." Some may identify depression with weakness; if so, avoid "setting them straight" at this point.)

2. **How do you think a depressed spouse would react to each of the following situations?**
    - **gaining 15 pounds**
      _____
    - **never hearing a compliment from his or her spouse**
      _____
    - **winning a new car**
      _____
    - **a sermon titled "Living in the Joy of the Lord"**
      _____
    - **losing his or her job**
      _____
    - **a spouse who says, "Let's go away for the weekend"**
      _____

(The first, second, and fifth events probably would deepen the person's sense of hopelessness. Winning a new car might lift the depression at first; if the depression is deep, however, the "bounce" could be only temporary. A sermon titled "Living in the Joy of the Lord" or an invitation to go away for the weekend might buoy the spirits of some mildly depressed people, but others would find the effort pointless and even annoying.)

3. **Which of the following do you think cause depression? Why?**
    ____ **a chemical imbalance**
    ____ **lack of faith**
    ____ **stress**
    ____ **self-centeredness**
    ____ **exhaustion**
    ____ **disappointment**
    ____ **other** _____

(Any of these factors can contribute to depression. It doesn't follow, though, that trying to have more faith or selflessness will make depression go away.

Since this is an opinion question, however, don't try to "correct" group members who say otherwise.)

4. **How can you tell whether your spouse is depressed?** _____

_____

(Frequently mentioned symptoms of depression include weight loss or gain, mood swings, suicidal thoughts, difficulty sleeping, lack of concentration, crying spells, intense sadness or self-doubt, and inability to enjoy favorite activities.)

_____

5. **If you were depressed, who would you tell about it? Why?** _____

_____

(Answers will vary. Note whether group members would tell their spouses; you may want to refer to this later.)

6. **If you were depressed, how do you think your spouse would respond?**

_____

(Answers will vary. If people think their spouses would respond negatively, observe that these reactions would be understandable rather than condemning them.)

**A lot of spouses wouldn't know how to respond to a depressed mate. Fortunately, we're about to get advice on that from three people who've been there.**

3. CATCHING THE VISION

## Watching and Discussing the DVD
*(20-25 minutes)*

After viewing the DVD, use questions like these to help participants think through what they saw and heard.

1. **What was your attitude toward depression before you watched this DVD segment? Did it change at all? If so, how? If not, why not?**

(Answers will vary; some group members may feel more empathy for depressed people or their spouses.)

2. **Which of the following symptoms of depression were mentioned in this video? How might someone first notice them in a spouse? Which ones would be easiest to ignore or dismiss? Why?**
    - **fatigue**
    - **weight loss or gain**
    - **mood swings**
    - **suicidal thoughts**
    - **difficulty sleeping**
    - **lack of concentration**
    - **crying spells**
    - **intense sadness or self-doubt**
    - **inability to enjoy favorite activities**

(All were mentioned. Perhaps the hardest symptoms to spot would be those that could be explained by other causes, or those that could be dismissed as "temporary.")

3. **How did Mitch Temple's depression affect his wife and children? Why was it still hard for him to see that he was depressed and to get the help he needed? On a scale of 1 to 10 (10 hardest), how difficult would it be for you to admit you were depressed? Why?**
(Because Mitch was moody, his wife never knew what to expect from him. She thought he didn't care about her anymore. Perhaps he didn't realize he was depressed because he'd struggled with the problem for many years, and had come to think of it as normal. Answers about the difficulty of admitting to being depressed will vary, but some probably will mention the stigma associated with depression—that depressed people are weak, self-absorbed, or spiritually deficient. Point out the value of ignoring those misconceptions and getting professional counseling for depression.)

4. **How did Mitch's wife contribute to his recovery? If you were depressed, how would you want your spouse to help you?**
(She had to learn what depression was and how it affects marriages. Instead of judging, she was there for Mitch, telling him she loved him and would stand

by him. That gave him strength to keep going. Answers to the second part of the question will differ, but some probably will recommend the attitude Mitch's wife displayed.)

5.  **What loss led to Dr. Gary Rosberg's depression? How was it different from normal grieving?**
    (Gary's father had died, and Gary hadn't gone through the usual grieving process. His unexpressed grief emerged in the form of depression.)

6.  **Barb Rosberg prayed that God would change the circumstances of her husband's life—but He didn't. What would you have done at that point? What did Barb do, and what was the result?**
    (Barb realized she had to change. She kept praying, asking God what to do. The actions group members would have taken will vary.)

7.  **Dr. Juli Slattery says that depression affects the way spouses communicate and the way they see each other. How would you expect a depressed person to communicate with and see his or her spouse? How would you expect the spouse to communicate with and see the depressed person?**
    (A depressed person might communicate less than usual or not at all, talk about the pointlessness of life or the desirability of death, or speak with little apparent emotion. He or she might believe the spouse lacked understanding or wanted to be rid of him or her. The spouse of a depressed person might see him or her as self-pitying or uncooperative, and out of frustration or fear, communicate harshly or as little as possible.)

8.  **If you had encountered Juli at church during her postpartum depression and asked, "How are you?" what do you think she would have replied? Why? How can a person make it easier for his or her spouse to be honest about being depressed?**
    (Unless you had a close and candid relationship with Juli, she might have said, "Fine," as people often do in order to be socially and spiritually acceptable. Spouses need to love each other unconditionally, in sickness and in health— and to prove through word and action that they'll accept each other no matter what.)

## Bible Study

*(10 minutes)*

Depending on your group's priorities and the time available, have volunteers read some or all of these Bible passages and discuss the questions that follow them.

> *Now Ahab told Jezebel everything Elijah had done and how he had killed all the prophets with the sword. So Jezebel sent a messenger to Elijah to say, "May the gods deal with me, be it ever so severely, if by this time tomorrow I do not make your life like that of one of them."*
>
> *Elijah was afraid and ran for his life. When he came to Beersheba in Judah, he left his servant there, while he himself went a day's journey into the desert. He came to a broom tree, sat down under it and prayed that he might die. "I have had enough, LORD," he said. "Take my life; I am no better than my ancestors." Then he lay down under the tree and fell asleep.*
>
> *All at once an angel touched him and said, "Get up and eat." He looked around, and there by his head was a cake of bread baked over hot coals, and a jar of water. He ate and drank and then lay down again.*
>
> *The angel of the LORD came back a second time and touched him and said, "Get up and eat, for the journey is too much for you." So he got up and ate and drank. Strengthened by that food, he traveled forty days and forty nights until he reached Horeb, the mountain of God. There he went into a cave and spent the night.*
>
> *And the word of the LORD came to him: "What are you doing here, Elijah?"*
>
> *He replied, "I have been very zealous for the LORD God Almighty. The Israelites have rejected your covenant, broken down your altars, and put your prophets to death with the sword. I am the only one left, and now they are trying to kill me too."*
>
> *The LORD said, "Go out and stand on the mountain in the presence of the LORD, for the LORD is about to pass by."*
>
> *Then a great and powerful wind tore the mountains apart and shattered the rocks before the LORD, but the LORD was not in the wind. After the wind there was an earthquake, but the LORD was not in the earthquake. After the earthquake came a fire, but the LORD was not in the fire. And after the fire came a gentle*

*whisper. When Elijah heard it, he pulled his cloak over his face and went out and stood at the mouth of the cave.*

*Then a voice said to him, "What are you doing here, Elijah?"*

*He replied, "I have been very zealous for the LORD God Almighty. The Israelites have rejected your covenant, broken down your altars, and put your prophets to death with the sword. I am the only one left, and now they are trying to kill me too."*

*The LORD said to him, "Go back the way you came, and go to the Desert of Damascus. When you get there, anoint Hazael king over Aram. Also, anoint Jehu son of Nimshi king over Israel, and anoint Elisha son of Shaphat from Abel Meholah to succeed you as prophet. Jehu will put to death any who escape the sword of Hazael, and Elisha will put to death any who escape the sword of Jehu. Yet I reserve seven thousand in Israel—all whose knees have not bowed down to Baal and all whose mouths have not kissed him." (1 Kings 19:1-18)*

1. **What symptoms of depression did Elijah have? What "treatment" did the angel and the Lord provide? How might a husband or wife do something similar for a depressed spouse?**

   (Elijah wanted to die; he thought the situation in Israel was hopeless. God met his physical needs with food and water, gave him a new mission, and assured him that he was not alone. A spouse might ensure that his or her partner's physical needs were met by taking him or her to the doctor; a spouse could help the depressed person discover a new direction in life; a spouse could assure the person that he or she was not alone.)

   *Then Job replied:*
   *"How long will you torment me and crush me with words?*
   *Ten times now you have reproached me; shamelessly you attack me.*
   *If it is true that I have gone astray, my error remains my concern alone.*
   *If indeed you would exalt yourselves above me and use my humiliation against me, then know that God has wronged me and drawn his net around me.*
   *"Though I cry, 'I've been wronged!' I get no response; though I call for help, there is no justice.*
   *He has blocked my way so I cannot pass; he has shrouded my paths in darkness." (Job 19:1-8)*

2. **How might this speech be worded if Job's situation had been one of the following? What would you do in each case if Job were your spouse?**
    - **if Job had lost his job a year before and hadn't been able to find a new one**
    - **if Job had just learned that he had multiple sclerosis**
    - **if Job had been imprisoned for a crime he didn't commit**
    - **if Job had just lost his six-year-old son in a car accident**

(Answers will vary. Much of Job's speech could remain the same in each case; he probably would still be weary of false comforters and feel that God had wronged him. In each case, a spouse could see that his physical needs were met, assure him that he wasn't alone, and help him to find a new direction.)

> My tears have been my food day and night, while men say to me all day long, "Where is your God?"
> These things I remember as I pour out my soul: how I used to go with the multitude, leading the procession to the house of God, with shouts of joy and thanksgiving among the festive throng.
> Why are you downcast, O my soul?
> Why so disturbed within me?
> Put your hope in God,
> for I will yet praise him,
> my Savior and my God.
> My soul is downcast within me;
> therefore I will remember you
> from the land of the Jordan,
> the heights of Hermon—from Mount Mizar. (Psalm 42:3-6)

3. **Would you say that the psalmist was depressed? Why or why not? What does he suggest as the solution? What might have happened if the psalmist's wife had bought a greeting card with this message on it and had given it to him?**

(The psalmist seems depressed, especially at the beginning. It might depend on how long he'd felt this way. His solution: to put his hope in God and praise Him. Getting this ultimately upbeat message might have appealed to the psalmist, but could just as easily have annoyed him if he'd gotten it from his wife. Depressed people can feel that others just don't understand, that they don't grasp the hopelessness of the situation.)

## Applying the Principles
*(10 minutes)*

Have group members turn to the "Making It Work" section in the Participant's Guide. Let them work individually, answering the question and writing notes to their spouses.

Participants may not want to share their answer or their notes; encourage them to give the notes to their spouses later.

If time allows, discuss the following:

**Let's say neither you nor your spouse has a problem with depression—at least not now. But that could change. What can you do to prepare for the possibility that one or both of you could someday be depressed?**

(Some possibilities: Learn all we can about depression; agree that if one of us becomes depressed, he or she will let the other know; find out how to contact a counselor in case we need one; keep communicating with each other about feelings; make sure each other's physical needs are met, that we know we're not alone, and that we have a purpose in life; pray for each other.)

## Reinforcing Your Point
*(5 minutes)*

In the Participant's Guide, this session's "Bringing It Home" section offers advice on what to do if your spouse needs psychological help. Encourage group members to read it later.

Remind spouses that if they need guidance on depression or living with a depressed mate and would like to speak with a therapist, Focus on the Family maintains a referral network of Christian counselors. For information, call 1-800-A-FAMILY and ask for the counseling department.

If your group is comfortable doing so, conclude by asking one or more volunteers to pray for couples who may be struggling with depression. You might want to conclude the prayers by reading Psalm 42:5:

**Why are you downcast, O my soul?**
**Why so disturbed within me?**
**Put your hope in God,**
**for I will yet praise him,**
**my Savior and my God.**

Session 6

# THE WONDERFUL WORLD OF FINANCES

No matter how the economy is doing, couples clash over cash—and credit, too. Family history, values, feelings about the future, self-discipline, self-esteem, and even math skills can contribute to the marital wealth wars.

In this DVD segment, popular author and broadcaster Dave Ramsey talks about the money myths, mysteries, and mechanics that can spell the difference between lifelong bickering and financial peace. Host Dr. Greg Smalley adds a true tale from his own marriage, and urges viewers to work on the core issues that often underlie budget battles.

## Session Aim
To help couples work together to make wise financial decisions—despite possible differences in their attitudes toward money.

## Setting the Stage
- Read this session plan and Chapter 6 in the Participant's Guide.
- Provide pencils or pens.
- If you want to use the "Budgets of Famous Couples" activity in Step 1, you may wish to recruit a "game show host" before the session—and bring a prize for the winning team.
- Cue up the DVD to segment 6, "The Wonderful World of Finances."

## Optional Icebreaker
*(5 minutes)*

Would you make a good game show host? If not, feel free to ask a more likely group member to take that role in the following optional opener.

Form teams. Say (or have your volunteer host say): **It's time to play Budgets of Famous Couples! I'm going to read you the monthly budgets of four well-known couples, and the first team to answer correctly wins that round. We'll have four rounds, and the team with the highest score at the end wins the game!**

**Here's an example. This famous couple has a monthly budget that looks like the following:**

| Sample Couple Monthly Budget | |
|---|---|
| Soot remover | $400 |
| Candy canes | $250 |
| Reindeer feed | $1,500 |
| Weight Watchers frozen entrees | $375 |

**Who is this famous couple?** (Santa Claus and Mrs. Claus.)
**Okay, that one was easy. Let's see how you do on the rest.**

Read the first of the following budgets and give teams a chance to answer. Work your way through all four and award prizes accordingly.

| Couple A Monthly Budget | |
|---|---|
| Blue hair dye | $25 |
| Beer | $250 |
| Donuts | $300 |
| Radiation detectors | $250 |
| (Answer: Homer and Marge of *The Simpsons*) | |

**Couple B Monthly Budget**

| | |
|---|---|
| Stretch pants | $900 |
| Scientific equipment | $5,000,000 |
| Transparent lipstick | $250 |
| Asbestos wallpaper | $1,800 |

(Answer: Reed and Sue Richards of the *Fantastic Four*)

**Couple C Monthly Budget**

| | |
|---|---|
| Sandwich rolls | $250 |
| Lunchmeat | $500 |
| Clothing | $2,500 |
| Hair wax | $75 |

(Answer: Dagwood and Blondie)

**Couple D Monthly Budget**

| | |
|---|---|
| Dog food | $35 |
| Tornado insurance | $300 |
| Farmhands | $5,000 |
| Home repairs | $7,500 |

(Answer: Auntie Em and Uncle Henry in *The Wizard of Oz*)

Congratulate the winning team. Then ask:

**What can you tell about a couple from the way it spends money?**

(What its priorities and values are, whether it's "successful," perhaps how the spouses were raised, etc.)

**What can you tell about a couple from the way it discusses money?**

(Differences in family backgrounds, one person's respect for the other, whether there might be a power struggle going on, etc.)

**You don't have to answer this out loud, but what could the rest of us tell from the way you and your spouse discuss money?**

**Many of us probably would rather not have an audience when we talk about money. Conflict over finances is one of the most common problems**

married couples face. In this session, you're going to hear from an expert on how you can fight that trend in your own relationship.

## Identifying Your Needs
*(5-10 minutes)*

Have group members turn to the "Finding Yourself" section in the Participant's Guide. Ask them to fill out individually the survey found there. People probably will be reluctant to share answers with the whole group, and might find themselves arguing if they discuss some of the questions as couples. For those reasons, talk about questions 4 and 6 as a group; encourage couples to discuss the rest at home. You may want to read through all the questions, though, and offer brief comments as follows.

1. **If a dollar bill reflected the way you and your spouse handle money, what might be the motto printed on it?**
   ___ **"In God we trust."**
   ___ **"Here today, gone tomorrow."**
   ___ **"You can't take that away from me."**
   ___ **"You're all I need."**
   ___ **"Caution: May cause violent behavior."**
   ___ other _____
   You and your spouse may have very different answers to this one. Rest assured that differing perspectives on finances aren't unusual, and don't in themselves mean that something is wrong with a marriage.

2. **Which of the following do you feel most confident about? Least confident? Does your spouse "take up the slack" in areas where you feel least confident? If so, how?**
   ___ **deciding to make a big purchase**
   ___ **balancing a checkbook**
   ___ **finding bargains**
   ___ **making investments**

\_\_\_ earning money
\_\_\_ paying bills
\_\_\_ keeping track of a budget
\_\_\_ other _____

When you discuss this one, you may want to ask your spouse whether he or she wants to take up that slack—or feels forced to do so. You may need to negotiate a fairer solution.

3. Which of the following did you and your spouse discuss before you got married? Which did you not discuss but wish you had?

\_\_\_ your financial goals
\_\_\_ your debt
\_\_\_ how you would use credit cards
\_\_\_ whether both spouses would work
\_\_\_ your family's attitude toward money
\_\_\_ your beliefs about giving money to the church

If you didn't talk about these things—and most couples probably didn't—there's still time.

4. How would you explain to a 10-year-old what "the value of a dollar" is? How does this compare to your spouse's answer? _____

_____

(Answers will vary. Adults usually don't use this phrase literally, but are referring to the need for children to understand the effort required to earn money.)

5. Name two necessities and two luxuries. How do your answers compare with those of your spouse? _____

_____

It's not uncommon for spouses to calibrate their "luxury detectors" differently. When you compare answers later, keep in mind that disagreeing isn't necessarily bad. It may give you a chance to learn the art of compromise.

6. What's the best thing you've done with money since you got married? What made it such a positive experience? _____

_____

(Answers will vary. Some might fondly remember helping someone in need, or creating a happy memory for their family, or making a wise purchase that lasted a long time. The point is that money isn't just a moral threat; it can be used for good, too. Couples can work together to make those positive experiences more frequent.)

## 3. CATCHING THE VISION

## Watching and Discussing the DVD
*(20-25 minutes)*

After viewing the DVD, use questions like these to help couples think through what they saw and heard.

1. **If you had a dollar for every time you and your spouse have disagreed about money, would you be rich? Why or why not?**
   (Probably not, though many couples may feel that way.)

2. **Do you agree with the following Dave Ramsey quotes? Why or why not?**
   - **"Money is not the problem. What we are really fighting about here is who is in control."**
   - **"Budgeting together creates communication and cooperation over some of life's difficult subjects."**
   - **"Debt places huge relational pressures on marriages. . . . There is a sense of futility, this sense I am going to go really hard and get nowhere."**

   (In the interest of time, you may want to take a vote by raising hands and ask dissenters to briefly explain their objections. The goal is to get people to think through what Dave Ramsey said, not to determine the correct position on each issue.)

3. **According to Dave, couples who fight about finances are really fighting about power, priorities, and passions. In which of those areas do you expect the most disagreement in the coming year? Why?**

(Answers will vary. You may want to remind participants that unless they can resolve their power struggle, conflict over how to spend their money will continue. They may need outside help with the power struggle, since the struggle itself will interfere with its resolution.)

4. **Which of the following do you think would create in a marriage what Dave calls a sense of infidelity or broken trust? How could that broken trust be restored?**
   - **having a checking account you haven't told your spouse about**
   - **forgetting to send in your car loan payment one month and keeping it a secret**
   - **running up $5,000 in credit card debt and not telling your spouse**
   - **promising your child a Disney World vacation without consulting your spouse**

   (Answers will vary, though any of these could damage trust. Honestly discussing financial expectations, plans, and mistakes over a long period of time would help restore a spouse's confidence.)

5. **If you spent only what you'd budgeted in writing beforehand, how much would you have spent last week? Do you regret any purchases you made? Why or why not?**
   (Chances are that group members wouldn't have been able to spend anything. If you've had buyer's remorse in the last week, or just realize you could have gone without something that seemed irresistible at the time, you might want to mention that.)

6. **Is your marriage made up of a "nerd" and a "free spirit"? If so, how does that work when it comes to finances? If not, how would you describe the personality types of your spouse and yourself when it comes to money?**
   (Note that "nerd" in this context isn't a slur; it's just a cautious, detail-oriented person. Since labeling each other's personality types in front of the group could embarrass some, you may want to have people discuss this as couples only.)

7. **According to Dave, "The preacher didn't pronounce you a joint venture. He said, 'Now you are one.'" What's the difference? How could it affect the way spouses plan their saving, spending, and giving?**

   (Joint ventures may require cooperation and compromise for the sake of a project's success, but "oneness" is a deeper, lifelong bond. That doesn't mean you never disagree, but it does mean you plan financially with the assumption that you'll stay together no matter how differently you see things and no matter how your plans pan out.)

8. **Do you have a "love drawer" in your home? If so, can you and your spouse name its contents? If not, can both of you name the locations of the documents that belong in that place?**

   (Answers will vary. Participants might not use Dave's system. But if they have an alternative, encourage them to describe it.)

## Bible Study
*(10 minutes)*

For additional biblical input on this subject, ask volunteers to read some or all of the following passages and discuss the questions that follow them.

> *The plans of the diligent lead to profit as surely as haste leads to poverty.*
> *A fortune made by a lying tongue is a fleeting vapor and a deadly snare. . . .*
> *If a man shuts his ears to the cry of the poor, he too will cry out and not be answered. . . .*
> *He who loves pleasure will become poor; whoever loves wine and oil will never be rich. . . .*
> *In the house of the wise are stores of choice food and oil, but a foolish man devours all he has.*
> *He who pursues righteousness and love finds life, prosperity and honor. . . .*
> *The sluggard's craving will be the death of him, because his hands refuse to work.*
> *All day long he craves for more, but the righteous give without sparing.*
> (Proverbs 21:5-6, 13, 17, 20-21, 25-26)

1. **How would you and your spouse distill these proverbs into "Seven Rules for Financial Stability" that you both agree on?**
   (Answers will vary, but here's one way to paraphrase these insights:
   1. Don't rush into buying or investing; take time to plan.
   2. Tell the truth, even if it means losing money.
   3. Share with the poor, or you could become one of them.
   4. There's no such thing as a free lunch, especially if it's all you can eat.
   5. Save for a rainy day.
   6. Do the right thing and you'll live long and prosper.
   7. It's better to give than to wish you'd receive.)

   *A good name is more desirable than great riches; to be esteemed is better than silver or gold.*
   *Rich and poor have this in common: The LORD is the Maker of them all.*
   *A prudent man sees danger and takes refuge, but the simple keep going and suffer for it.*
   *Humility and the fear of the LORD bring wealth and honor and life. . . .*
   *The rich rule over the poor, and the borrower is servant to the lender. . . .*
   *A generous man will himself be blessed, for he shares his food with the poor. . . .*
   *He who oppresses the poor to increase his wealth and he who gives gifts to the rich—both come to poverty. . . .*
   *Do not exploit the poor because they are poor and do not crush the needy in court, for the LORD will take up their case and will plunder those who plunder them. . . .*
   *Do not be a man who strikes hands in pledge or puts up security for debts; if you lack the means to pay, your very bed will be snatched from under you.*
   *(Proverbs 22:1-4, 7, 9, 16, 22-23, 26, 27)*

2. **How would you and your spouse distill these proverbs into "Nine Financial Commandments" that you both agree on?**
   (Answers will differ, but here's one possibility:
   1. Don't trade your reputation for money.
   2. Don't think that having money makes you better than anyone else.
   3. If something looks risky, it probably is.
   4. If you want real prosperity, remember that it's not about you.

5. Borrowing makes debt your boss.

6. When it comes to generosity, what goes around comes around.

7. Using or bribing people won't really help you get ahead.

8. Don't treat the poor as enemies, because God is their Friend.

9. Don't assume you'll be able to pay off that loan someday.)

*Keep your lives free from the love of money and be content with what you have, because God has said, "Never will I leave you; never will I forsake you." (Hebrews 13:5)*

3. **How does the second half of this verse explain the reason for the first half? If a husband and wife don't agree on the second half, can they agree on the first? If they do agree on the second half, will they necessarily obey the first? Why or why not?**

(Since God promises to provide for our real needs, we're to spurn looking for more and more money. It's possible to avoid materialism whether or not you believe God will take care of you, though it's probably not easy. If you *really* believe God will take care of you, you won't chase wealth or possessions; if your agreement with the idea is superficial or halfhearted, it may make little or no difference in your behavior.)

## 5. MAKING IT WORK

### Applying the Principles

*(10 minutes)*

Have group members turn to the "Making It Work" section in the participant's guide. Let people complete the activity as individuals, then get together as couples to compare answers and "sell" each other on their favorite financial tips from the list.

Then, as a group, discuss questions like the following.

**How did your "selling" go?**

(Affirm any couples who at least tried the process, whether or not they seemed to succeed.)

**Would this process of narrowing down options, working on differences by convincing each other, and voting on a plan help you deal with financial questions? If not, what would you suggest?**

(People may wonder what they're supposed to do in case of a tie. Possibilities include gathering more information on the options, allowing more time to convince each other, and bringing in a third party to provide fresh perspective or even "binding arbitration" if both spouses agree to it.)

**Do you think you'll actually follow any of the tips on the list? Why or why not?**

(Answers will vary. If some people don't like the ideas on the list, encourage them to share one or two of their own.)

**Have you followed some of them already? If so, what happened?**

## Reinforcing Your Point
*(5 minutes)*

Remind group members to read the "Bringing It Home" section of their Participant's Guides later this week. In it, a psychologist explains how couples can decide together how much to spend.

To wrap up this session, try comments like the following.

**Finances are complicated. It would take a lot longer than we have today to understand everything from budgeting to bond markets. But there are plenty of financial advisors out there, as well as books on the subject.**

One book you may want to recommend is *Complete Guide to Faith-Based Family Finances* by Ron Blue with Jeremy L. White (Focus on the Family/Tyndale House Publishers, 2008). The following advice is adapted from that book.

**If you and your spouse have a difference of opinion on finances, try approaching conflict with one or more of these guidelines in mind:**
- **Stick to the problem at hand.**
- **Get on the same side of the fence.**
- **Try to identify the core issue.**
- **Don't be a mind reader.**

- **Don't let the sun go down on your anger.**
- **Avoid character assassination.**
- **Never forget that your relationship with your spouse is far more important than "winning" an argument or "being right."**
- **Remember that love keeps no record of wrongs.**

Point out that these tips come not from a counselor but a financial expert—Ron Blue. He and his wife, Judy, have used strategies like these "to help prevent communication stalemates, blowouts, and breakdowns."

**Here's how Ron puts it: "In order to maintain our commitment to love, cherish, and honor our spouses, we need to yield ourselves and our rights, first to God and then to one another."**

**That's sound advice, whether the subject is money or not. In fact, it's a pretty good summary of the sessions we've spent together.**

Before closing with prayer, remind group members that when they need help to solve a marital problem, it's available from one or more Christian counselors in your area. If your church recommends one, provide contact information. Otherwise, encourage people to call Focus on the Family, which maintains a referral network of Christian counselors. For information, group members can call 1-800-A-FAMILY and ask for the counseling department. They can also download free, printable brochures offering help for couples at http://www.focusonthefamily.com/marriage/articles/brochures.aspx.

# About Our DVD Presenters
## *Essentials of Marriage: Handle with Care*

After suffering the loss of a $4 million real estate portfolio, **Dave Ramsey** decided to return to the basics of personal finance and help others. Dave is the author of the New York Times best-selling books *Financial Peace* and *The Total Money Makeover*. He is also the host of the nationally syndicated *Dave Ramsey Show*. Many national corporations as well as tens of thousands of individuals have benefited from his Financial Peace University program and his live seminars. He and his wife, Sharon, live in Nashville and have three children.

**Dr. John Trent** is president of the Center for Strong Families and StrongFamilies.com, an organization that trains leaders to launch and lead marriage and family programs in their churches and communities. John speaks at conferences across the country and has written or cowritten more than a dozen award-winning and bestselling books, including *The 2 Degree Difference* and the million-selling parenting classic *The Blessing* with Gary Smalley. His books, of which there are more than two million in print, have been translated into 11 languages. John has been a featured guest on radio and television programs including *Focus on the Family, The 700 Club*, and CNN's *Sonya Live in L.A.* John and his wife, Cindy, have been married for 28 years and have two daughters.

**Dr. Archibald Hart** is well known for his ministry to churches through psychological training, education, and consultation. A former dean of the School of Psychology at Fuller Theological Seminary, he is now retired from full-time teaching but continues to examine issues of stress, depression, and anxiety. Dr. Hart is the author of 24 books, including *Thrilled to Death, Stressed or Depressed*, and *Safe Haven Marriage*. Dr. Hart and his wife, Kathleen, live in California. They have three daughters and seven grandchildren.

Since founding Precept Ministries International with her husband, Jack, in 1970 with the vision to establish people in God's Word, international Bible teacher and four-time Gold Medallion award-winning author **Kay Arthur** has written more than 100 books and Bible studies. Kay is also the teacher and host of *Precepts for Life*, a radio and television program that reaches a worldwide viewing audience of over 94 million, teaching them how to discover truth for themselves. Today, God is using Precept Ministries to reach nearly 150 countries with inductive Bible studies translated into nearly 70 languages. Kay serves as executive vice president and shares the office of Precept CEO with Jack. The Arthurs live in Chattanooga, Tennessee.

**Dr. Gary and Barb Rosberg**, cofounders of America's Family Coaches, host a nationally syndicated daily radio program and have conducted conferences on marriage and family relationships in more than 100 cities across the country. The Rosbergs have written more than a dozen prominent marriage and family resources, including *The 5 Love Needs of Men & Women* (a Gold Medallion finalist) and *Divorce-Proof Your Marriage* (a Gold Medallion winner). Gary earned his Ed.D. from Drake University and has been a marriage and family counselor for more than 25 years. Married more than 30 years, the Rosbergs live outside Des Moines, Iowa, and have two married daughters and four grandchildren.

**Dr. Greg Smalley** earned his doctorate in clinical psychology from Rosemead School of Psychology at Biola University. He also holds master's degrees in counseling psychology (Denver Seminary) and clinical psychology (Rosemead School of Psychology). Greg is president of Smalley Marriage Institute, a marriage and family ministry in Branson, Missouri, and serves as chairman of the board of the National Marriage Association. Greg has published more than 100 articles on parenting and relationship issues. He is the coauthor of *The DNA of Parent-Teen Relationships* (with his father, Gary Smalley) and *The Men's Relational Toolbox* (with his father and his brother, Michael). Greg, his wife, Erin, and their three children live in Branson, Missouri.

**Gary Thomas** is a writer and the founder/director of the Center for Evangelical Spirituality, a speaking and writing ministry that combines Scripture, history, and the Christian classics. His books include *Sacred Marriage, Authentic Faith* (winner of the Gold Medallion award in 2003), and *Seeking the Face of God*. Gary has spoken in 49 states and four countries and has served as the campus pastor at Western Seminary, where he is an adjunct professor. Gary, his wife, Lisa, and their three kids live in Bellingham, Washington.

**Dr. Julianna Slattery** is a family psychologist for Focus on the Family. Juli is the author of *Finding the Hero in Your Husband, Guilt-Free Motherhood,* and *Beyond the Masquerade*. Applying biblical wisdom to the everyday lives of women and families is her passion. She shares her message with a combination of humor, candor, and foundational truth. Juli earned a doctor of psychology and master of science in clinical psychology at Florida Institute of Technology, a master of arts in psychology from Biola University, and a bachelor of arts from Wheaton College. Juli and her husband, Mike, live in Colorado Springs and are the parents of three boys.

**Mitch Temple** is a licensed marriage and family therapist and author of *The Marriage Turnaround*. He holds two graduate degrees, in ministry and in marriage and family therapy, from Southern Christian University. Mitch currently serves as the director of the marriage department at Focus on the Family in Colorado Springs. He has conducted intensives nationwide for couples on the brink of divorce and has served as a family, pulpit, and counseling minister in churches for a total of 23 years. He was director of pastoral care, small groups, family ministry, and a counseling center at a large church for 13 years. He and his wife, Rhonda, have been married for more than 24 years and have three children.

# FOCUS ON THE FAMILY®

## Welcome to the Family

Whether you purchased this book, borrowed it, or received it as a gift, we're glad you're reading it. It's just one of the many helpful, encouraging, and biblically based resources produced by Focus on the Family® for people in all stages of life.

Focus began in 1977 with the vision of one man, Dr. James Dobson, a licensed psychologist and author of numerous best-selling books on marriage, parenting, and family. Alarmed by the societal, political, and economic pressures that were threatening the existence of the American family, Dr. Dobson founded Focus on the Family with one employee and a once-a-week radio broadcast aired on 36 stations.

Now an international organization reaching millions of people daily, Focus on the Family is dedicated to preserving values and strengthening and encouraging families through the life-changing message of Jesus Christ.

## Focus on the Family MAGAZINES

These faith-building, character-developing publications address the interests, issues, concerns, and challenges faced by every member of your family from preschool through the senior years.

| FOCUS ON THE FAMILY® MAGAZINE | FOCUS ON THE FAMILY CLUBHOUSE JR.® Ages 4 to 8 | FOCUS ON THE FAMILY CLUBHOUSE® Ages 8 to 12 | FOCUS ON THE FAMILY CITIZEN® U.S. news issues |
|---|---|---|---|

## For More INFORMATION

 **ONLINE:**
Log on to
FocusOnTheFamily.com
In Canada, log on to
FocusOnTheFamily.ca

 **PHONE:**
Call toll-free:
800-A-FAMILY
(232-6459)
In Canada, call toll-free:
800-661-9800

Rev. 12/08

# More Great Resources
## from Focus on the Family®

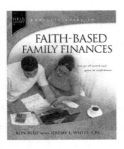

### Complete Guide to Faith-Based Family Finances
By Ron Blue and Jeremy White
Whether you're a financial whiz, a financial novice, or somewhere in between, the *Complete Guide to Faith-Based Family Finances* is filled with commonsense, practical tools to help you make wise financial decisions year after year. In addition to covering every area of financial planning, this helpful resource contains the answers to many of the questions asked by families like yours. Hardcover.

### The Way to Love Your Wife: Creating Greater Love and Passion in the Bedroom
By Clifford L. Penner, Ph.D. and Joyce J. Penner, M.N., R.N.
*The Way to Love Your Wife* is a book on marital sex directed to men with the purpose of changing their attitude and approach toward sex. It helps take the pressure off of both spouses to perform or achieve certain results and gives the man the confidence he needs to know and understand how to meet his wife's needs. By doing so, both husband and wife will find sex more fulfilling. Paperback.

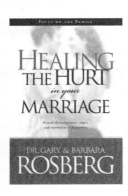

### Healing the Hurt in Your Marriage: Beyond Discouragement, Anger, and Resentment to Forgiveness
By Dr. Gary and Barbara Rosberg
Learn how to close the loop on unresolved conflict by practicing forgiving love. Marriage experts Dr. Gary and Barbara Rosberg draw from biblical wisdom to offer a step-by-step process that will move you beyond conflict to restore hope, harmony, and intimacy in your marriage today. Paperback.

## FOR MORE INFORMATION

 **Online:**
Log on to FocusOnTheFamily.com
In Canada, log on to focusonthefamily.ca.

 **Phone:**
Call toll free: 800-A-FAMILY
In Canada, call toll free: 800-661-9800.

BPZZXP1